I0475444

A Career In Trucking

Find Out if You Are The Right Type of Person To Enjoy Life as A Trucker.

Written by:
The Crazy Trucker

© 2011 www.Lifeasatrucker.com

www.lifeasatrucker.com

Disclaimer

This information is to be used as a tool to give you insight to answer your questions and empower you to ask other questions so you may use in making your own decisions about your life.

Hervy (The Crazy Trucker) will not be held responsible for any harm or liability you incur as a result of reading, watching, listening to any materials of any form in this book or on any of his websites, cds, dvds, videos, pdfs, or on any other products that he produces, distributes, sells or gives away. (Now that is a sentence!)

Materials produced and information given is done with the best intentions for the reader. Things change and you are encouraged to fact check information before you take action.

Many opinions offered are based upon logic, common sense, past experience, driver feedback, and combining information from various sources to create a big picture view useful for arriving at an opinion. (Forest as opposed to tree view...)

If you feel that the opinions presented may cause you harm don't follow them, as they are only opinions of the author and not a concrete directive for you to follow without regard to your own personal situation.

Don't quit your job or leave your wife talking about the book made you do it!

This disclaimer is done as a precaution in recognition of the current reality of a highly litigious society. Sad isn't it?

Just saying, anytime you can spill coffee on yourself and sue the restaurant because it is hot, and the judge not kick it out, you got to wonder..... what's next!

You should research information that you get from any source before you make important decisions in life, which includes, but is not limited to choosing a career.

In other words use common sense along with this book. Take what is relevant and ignore what is not. You are about to enter a new world, Enjoy!

www.lifeasatrucker.com

Message From The Author

A Special Thanks To...

Jimmy , Nick V, Dennis, Carl , Jennifer, Keith, Robin, Jeff, Anonymous, trucker wives, and many others for helping to make lifeasatrucker.com a site where you can feel at home and get information and support. New drivers, old drivers, trucker's wives, those thinking of becoming truck drivers, and those simply interested in who truckers are all are helped by your gift of time and knowledge.

If I forgot you, don't worry, I will mention you in the next publication! In the Mean time, Thanks So Much!

Back to The Soon To Be Truckers

After reading this book, if you are still interested in becoming a trucker, you should visit your nearest truck stop to pick up some free magazines which advertise trucking jobs.

Many of the trucking companies that advertise in these magazines will have their phone numbers and also a map detailing what area they are hiring in and what areas their trucks run.

(You'll learn why that could matter in the book)

Of course you can also <u>find trucking jobs online</u>. You will be able to search for jobs hiring in specific areas which makes it easier and faster.

Having the magazines, however, can be convenient to take to places where you don't want to carry a laptop or can't get a signal.

Make a list of trucking companies your interested in. Go back to the truck stop and see if there are drivers there for that company who lives near the area. The feedback about home time and miles from him/her is likely to be more accurate than someone who lives on the other side of the country or in a different proximity to the lanes of operation.

I have created pages at the back of this book for your notes.

If you want updated information, to find a trucking school, find a trucking job, answers and opinions about trucking, feel free to check out our website at <u>www.lifeasatrucker.com</u>

Table of Contents

Page   Content

www.lifeasatrucker.com

Who Are Truckers?

Truckers are people like Jimmy who drove 30 plus years before retiring and now still gives of his time educating others wanting to get into trucking. Truckers are people like Nick V, who get hired after months of trying but never gave up and got his chance. Now he is a trainer and frequent contributor online giving advice and encouragement to others. People like Carl, Dennis, Keith, Maya, Jeff, who have all given back to the up and coming. Larry An owner operator in Dallas have answered calls from people who are thinking of becoming o/o's to give advice. That's who trucker are.

Drivers come from all backgrounds and professions. You'll find ex dentists, doctors, accountants, welders, printers, painter, models, pro ball players, plumbers and brick masons, factory workers, printers, farmers, etc.

Some truckers are retired military, police officers or firemen. Truckers are also writers, poets, singers, songwriters, wrestlers, inventors and savvy businessmen.

www.lifeasatrucker.com

Truckers were predominately Caucasian males back in the day, but today most trucking companies are a melting pot of cultures and races. Many trucking companies are also courting women to join their team.   Some reports have shown women to be safer drivers because they are less aggressive.

For those who may be hesitant to join the ranks because of race, gender or size (as long as your healthy) please know that you will be welcomed by most trucking companies and other drivers so that shouldn't be a reason that you dismiss the idea of becoming a driver.

However, there are other reasons that you may not be ready to become a truck driver, and that is the reason that I wrote this book. Becoming a driver without the proper insight to make a decision depending on your specific circumstances could result in you being a miserable person on the road. It could even destroy your family and/or career and that is what we don't want to happen.   So let's get into the fun stuff!

www.lifeasatrucker.com

Are You The Type For The Trucking Lifestyle?

You need to be a certain type of person to be compatible for the trucking lifestyle in order to make trucking a career you love and respect and not just a job you end up hating.

Let's explore some of these qualities that you need to have.

1.   **A driver needs to be Self Reliant** – Able to carry out tasks without someone constantly micro managing from the office. You are basically given your pick up or delivery information and expected to plan your trip as needed to be on time. Some companies will provide the routing and some will not. Some companies will have GPS most still don't. GPS does not always provide good information for a truck so you still will need to have the ability to question strange directions and ultimately find where you are going. Don't worry school will teach you to read a map.

www.lifeasatrucker.com

Sometimes the address or phone number given from the company may be wrong. Often times finding the correct information yourself will be a lot quicker than calling the office for the information. You will need to do a lot of thinking for yourself as you encounter questionable situations. You may not believe it but some shippers can't even give directions to where they are located and some shippers or receivers at the border towns don't even speak or understand English. In these cases you can wait around on someone else to come around to interpret or find out yourself how to get there.

Tip: The internet or 1-800-free-411. Police, fire department, and taxi drivers can also help you to find addresses that won't show up on the internet or if you don't have access on the phone. Or Google their address.

2. **A Person Needs To Be Responsible** – You need to understand that pick up and delivery times are important and conduct yourself accordingly.

Oversleeping, not feeling like getting up, not noticing the time are not acceptable excuses for not making scheduled appointments. The last time I missed a scheduled delivery time, it keep me from getting good loads for a month.

I had too much faith in my internal clock which usually woke me up an hour before the alarm every morning. I didn't bother to charge my phone. Because of that, the alarm didn't work and my internal clock didn't either. I didn't wake up until after the scheduled appointment.

Ever remember going to the store to pick something up when they said it would be there and it wasn't? Ever asked about merchandise and they said the truck didn't come in? You ask, "Do you know when it will be in?" They say, "When the truck gets here, I don't know when that will be." Often our arrival has an impact on companies doing business on the retail side or in the manufacturing process which means arriving late costs them money.

It could also lead to them having unhappy customers which will make them your company's unhappy customer. Of course that means your company may be unhappy with you! Even worse, suppose the contract is lost. Your company will need less drivers. See where this is going?

Tip: Be proactive. It's nice that you have confidence in yourself like I did, but don't rely on past performance when there are tools (such as alarms) to make sure you wake up. I should have just charged the phone in my case and I never would have been late.

3. **A driver needs to be a people person** – Many truckers like the open road and solitude of being a trucker, but he or she should still have good social skills. They will be needed. Developing a good relationship with the dispatcher or driver manager is essential for a productive and prosperous career. As a driver you should also be able to have a pleasant interaction with the shippers and receivers. They indirectly keep you employed.

www.lifeasatrucker.com

Sometimes their attitude or work ethic may not be the best but it is in your best interest to be tolerant (using good, mature, adult discretion) and remain positive using a little patience. (Ok, sometimes a lot of patience!)

They are in the position of leverage. Sometimes your attitude (even if you only reflect back to them what you are getting) may cost you extra time at the dock. Besides, if you remain pleasant and cordial often you will see a change in their attitude as they realize that you are not the person who put them in that childish, unpleasant mood. You become therapeutic to them and they can do a 180 degree change from hateful and unpleasant to friendly and accommodating.

It's amazing when this happens. It's like you just won a battle while armed but never firing a shot. (Aware of ignorance but in control of your response to it)

You'll find this often in life.

www.lifeasatrucker.com

Your smile and positive attitude can make things happen when you don't expect it.

Sometimes you might encounter an attitude problem with your own dispatcher. Handle it the same way. He or she deals with a lot of people some of which won't be pleasant to him/her. People sometimes let others ruin their mood and so they take it out on the next person. It's easy to eventually come across a bad attitude. Don't take it personal unless repeated offenses prove it to be personal and then be tactful about addressing their behavior toward you.

How well you interact with people will have an impact on how well you like your job and how much you enjoy life!

4. **A driver needs to be a Good Communicator** – Many companies have a policy for you to call in every morning when you are out by a certain time. It may depend on what your hauling or who your hauling for. Some shippers may want to keep track of the shipment in order to update their customers.

In either case, it doesn't matter, it's all a part of the job.

You are in possession of expensive equipment and freight. Plus your dealing with people who may need the product you have in order to plan. If they ask you to call, do so. If you don't, they may call you. If they call you don't get upset and rude.

You will hear drivers talking to other drivers sometimes about how they cursed out or hung up on their dispatcher or shipper because he/she called to see where they were. That's ridiculous! Guys with that attitude are the same ones complaining about getting low miles every week.

If you owned a trucking company and had a driver who you hadn't heard from all day hauling freight your company is responsible for you might call too. Right?

Tip: Sometimes all we have to do is role reversal and look at things from more than just our point of view to see if something we are experiencing actually makes sense or whether we should be offended. Role reversal would often keep us from overreacting. (For trucking and in life.)

Soon all trucks and trailers will probably be tracked electronically anyway. Regardless, communication is very important.

You also need to let them know your ETA (estimated time of arrival) or empty time so that you can be dispatched on your next load. Otherwise, you could end up sitting empty, waiting for them to find you another load. Waiting is lost productivity which means less money for you both.

Be sure to call the shippers or receivers when you see that you will be late or early. Sometimes you may get a load that delivers far later than you are able to arrive. I always call and see can if it can be delivered early. If they say yes, let your dispatcher know so he or she can plan your next load accordingly.

Tip: Communication is important in trucking but it is also in building relationships in life. Relationships are important cornerstones to success, prosperity and happiness, whether you are trucking or not.

www.lifeasatrucker.com

Note – By default the better you are at communicating and building healthy relationships, the better you can handle stress and the more defense you have against depression, diseases and even ending up in poverty.

5. **A driver needs to be Trustworthy** – There will be times that you will have access to sensitive information, restricted areas, high dollar freight, etc. You will likely have access to personal belongings at your home terminal and at companies that you visit. You may be given keys and passwords to company gates of yards with loaded trailers and equipment after hours.

This is one reason why, *some companies will be selective* based on your criminal background. They are protecting themselves from potential liability. Just as you would do it you were the owner of the company, especially if the insurance company or lawyers demanded it.

Important Advice For Those in Relationships

Trucking will put a strain on the best of relationships. If your relationship is on shaky ground, trucking can easily destroy it all together. If your relationship is not healthy, you may want to think twice about becoming a trucker.

For some who are experiencing problems at home, it may seem like a good idea to put the space between you to avoid arguments or disagreements.

For most couples, using trucking to create space would only amount to running from the real problems which should be addressed instead of ignored because the distance apart would only make things worst. I have seen many relationships ruined by trucking because of that separation. When this happens often trucking is the sole blame and the real issues just might go on with the individual into the next relationship. Why not go ahead and handle the real problem early on. Save the marriage.

So the lesson is.....

Realistically evaluate the condition of your relationship.

Are there trust issues? Any history of infidelity?
Do either of you give the other a reason for
suspicion of cheating?

If so trucking will help to magnify those trust issues.

Do you and your spouse both give love, affection, and
behave with the each other's feelings in mind?
(If yes, beautiful, congratulations!)
If... either of you self centered and demanding?

One sided relationships are tough. A self centered person
matched with a selfless person may survive sometimes but
it is not ideal for a healthy relationship. Both people should
be considerate and giving toward each other to build
strong foundations needed in a long distant relationship.

www.lifeasatrucker.com

Trucking will enable the self centered or self absorbed person to completely forget about the other person while 1,000's of miles away. If you are the self centered person as the driver, you can easily become preoccupied with the trucking lifestyle and your spouse will feel alone and abandoned. If you are extremely self centered and really just don't care, I would advise counseling not trucking.

If you decide to become a trucker and maintain a relationship with someone you don't care about or that doesn't care about you, you are asking for drama.

Money also causes many problems in relationships. Money is not as abundant in trucking for new drivers as advertisements would have you believe. (Avg. $30,000)

If you are reckless with your money as a trucker, you can easily spend half of your check or more every week living on the road. You must be intentional about controlling your spending habits. It's wise to keep a budget on the road. Write down every purchase you make 1st 3 months.

Your spouse can easily cause money problems too if she is at home spending money instead of paying bills. You need to be realistic about the type of spouse you have at home. If this was a problem that rarely occurred I would not mention it. Sometimes the wife's outrageous shopping, partying or other bad habits consumes the bill money and the bills are not paid. You should already have an idea, if your wife is like this. If she is, be alarmed and forewarned. DO NOT send your entire checks home!

Advice From Other Truckers in Successful Marriages

You'll hear many couples who are happy, talking about key components in the relationship that keeps the relationship strong. Watch the interviews with Larry and another one with Keith as they talk about how they maintain their relationships and keep a happy home.

*One word to look out for....***communication.***

http://relationships.lifeasatrucker.org

The Spouse of a Trucker

Not only must YOU be the right type of person for the trucking lifestyle but your spouse needs to be the right type of person also. She needs to be somewhat independent or self reliant, responsible and trustworthy.

Unpredictable things can come up at home and you won't be able to come home to handle them. Sometimes you may not even be reachable by phone immediately. (take a look at your phone service coverage maps, yes, there are still places where coverage is spotty).

If your spouse is not able to take care of herself and the family, she will live in constant stress especially after that first emergency happens which you are not there for.

Tip: Arrange for one of your friends to come to your spouses aid, in emergencies when your out of town when her normal backup is missing or insufficient.

Be proactive when possible to provide a sense of security and minimize stress to her even while your gone.

*Example: If the spouse is driving an old beat up car with one tire in the junkyard, get her AAA or TVC car club membership. This way, if she breaks down, she will be taken care of without having to figure out what to do next. Also go over these scenarios and **discuss** what to do next!*

If she is always calling you as if you can take care of things over the phone (as opposed to seeking your comfort or support to deal with issues, which you should cheerfully give), you will experience constant stress over the road. This can affect your sleeping, focus, memory, relationship and ultimately your health. These things being affected also makes you a hazard on the road and could cause you to have poor job performance.

She needs to be confident, independent and secure because if she is easily influenced by her friends, she could easily end up doubting your actions ...

...like failing to make it home when you thought you would be able to.

Your thinking, "well how do you know there will be times in which I will not be able to make it home when planned?"

The answer......because that is the nature of the job. Trucking is somewhat unpredictable, you are driving 2,000 to 3,500 miles per week across country, delivering and picking up freight, anything can happen to interrupt the trip and delay progress.

For instance, If you are in Las Cruses, NM headed back home in NC and you breakdown on Thursday in Sweetwater TX and can't get the part until the next day, you may not make it home until Tuesday because the shop may not work on the weekend or they may not get you in the bay until Monday. Is she going to believe that?

www.lifeasatrucker.com

That all depends on the dynamics of your relationship prior to trucking. The level of trust and integrity you have.

If you have a strong healthy relationship and you both are trustworthy and trusting, communicate well and put each others feelings in front of your own, then you have less to worry about because your likely to have a solid foundation that a relationships should be built on. For many people in new relationships today, this may not be the case yet.

Entertainment often shows cheating spouses like it is no big deal. Celebs and government officials playing around outside of their marriages are also common news stories. Of course there were also a few truckers before you with bad reps too. Those stories get spread like wildflowers. All of this in the subconscious mind can precondition people to be skeptical of their spouse from the start.

In any case, in relationships there are flaws, make sure you seriously address the issues if any, that exists in yours and be realistic on whether you being away from home for weeks at a time will make things better or worse for *your* relationship, not if it will make YOU happy to get away. If you don't care about the relationship, please don't just drag her along because you can. (Let her go.)

It isn't very considerate and Karma will not favor you. When she figures out your wasting her time and abusing her kindness or love, I hope she is not in your house and raising your kids or taking care of your elderly parents because then there is another level of problems.

We all have to do better in relationships today. Too many people just don't care about how they treat each other. If you need more insight of how driver's actions could impact relationships read the complaints of trucker wives. This will help you be a better partner over the road.

Anyone that has tried to have relationship with someone who has been terribly mistreated should know how serious of an impact this could have on a person. It trickles down and get's carried as baggage and all people after has to deal with it.

This is one of the primary reasons that relationships can be so difficult in today's time. Hopefully we will realize the need and develop the heart to start treating each other better. If not, eventually you might reap what you sow.

Get Her On Board

So your still here, great! The relationship is strong enough and you have the right type of spouse to be able to endure the trucking lifestyle, but just because you think she can handle it doesn't mean she will go for it. She might look at you like your crazy when you say, "I'm thinking of becoming a trucker". Just wait until you say you will be gone for 3 or 4 weeks at a time! You want your spouse on your team.

You need to get her on board. She needs to agree with you about taking on this challenging lifestyle. Some men may feel that they don't need their wives consent to become a trucker. They feel it's their right as a man to simply state how all things will be and then execute.

 www.lifeasatrucker.com

Becoming a trucker changes the entire dynamics of the family. It forces a spouse and children, if there are any, to change their lifestyle too.

It's a big deal, and most normal people would not want their significant other to make these types of decisions on his/her own and without his/her consent. Any doubts, switch the roles, wouldn't it bother you if your spouse did this to you?

You should get her to understand your plans. Detail how trucking will help your family in the long run. It can be a positive move and also not a permanent one if you develop and plan a course of action.

You can get into trucking, get experience while saving your money to buy a truck or drive while building a home business with your spouse. Maybe you will drive until you find a local or regional trucking job so that you are at home more often.

You may get her into <u>training as a freight broker</u> or
dispatcher and you two together can start a small trucking
or delivery company. My point is there are options that
could enable you to eventually come off the road. You
have to think it out and make plans. Set your goals.

One reason you need her to get on board is simple.
Supposed trucking is harder than you expect? Supposed
you hate the company you end up working for? Suppose
trucking causes unpredicted problems in the relationship
or problems come up at home after you get on the road.
Supposed you and her end up miserable.

If you agree about pursuing trucking together, you work
through the the problems together like a team. If you
forced her into the trucking lifestyle by leaving against her
wishes, there may (more like will) be a lot of resentment
by her because in her eyes **you** caused these problems
and **you** put this strain on your family. She may feel that
you don't even care. (women often think differently and
based on emotions not logic)

On bad days after dealing with accidents, ill attitudes, traffic jams, getting lost, etc and wanting to talk will she want to hear it? If the road keeps you from getting home for an event will she want to hear it? She won't always get it unless your able to take her on the road for a while. (Even valid points won't fly) She is dealing with her side of the issue which wouldn't be happening if you had not become a trucker in her eyes. How trucking was introduced into the relationship will determine how all of this drama is absorbed and processed. Oh, now you see!

It makes a difference to decide together!

Hopefully you can see that there will be much better harmony and peace for both of you if you decide together to engage in the trucking lifestyle.

Tip: Just my little 2 cents. Relationships are give and take. It requires sacrifices and even compromises by both parties at times. Besides, people eventually get tired of dictators. Jody, Judy or an internal uprising will eventually overthrow the regime of relentless dictatorship!

A Warning For Truckers About Being Away From Home

Note of caution: Some drivers feel that since they will be away from home, they can start relationships out of town and not worry about them being discovered by their spouse.   Don't fall in this trap!

Note: Truckers have a bad reputation because of this. Most people assume that most truckers are this way. There is only a fraction who would do this, but of course negativity and drama spreads much more rapidly than the opposite. This assumption is another reason why relationships are particularly hard for truck drivers.

You can only carry on like this for so long before things are out of hand. There may never be solid proof of cheating but it will show in your attitude or diminishing attention given to home. Which **is** solid proof (though not physical) that something is not right. What do you think that does to a relationship?

www.lifeasatrucker.com

It may also show in your growing distrust of your spouse as a result of **your** cheating. Eventually, guilt destroys the marriage or forces a confession in an attempt to save the marriage, which assures no guarantee. It's not an easy thing to do, especially if your still over the road and away from home. Again, reverse the roles, put yourself in her shoes.

Maybe a God loving, old school traditional values woman who remembers the good times together combined with your positive attributes prior to the mistake will agree to work on the marriage. **Still**, that won't erase the pain or damage from violation of trust. Only time along with appropriate remorse, the right attitude and meticulous nurturing can heal the wounds.

This means just because the will and desire is there to mend the relationship does not make success automatic. It's best to avoid ending up having to deal with this situation in the first place. (Don't cheat.)

Even worse has happened though, sometimes there **is solid proof** of cheating. Birth of a child, disease, phone calls from the deranged mistress are all real stories that I have heard more than once out here.

Sometimes temptation wins over at vulnerable moments, which we all experience. We have to know ourselves and avoid what may be too much of a challenge.

Other times the grass seems greener I suppose. Especially if a spouse is slacking or there is problem. Since we are not perfect, relationship won't be perfect either, and they will require a lot of work. Just like jumping trucking company to trucking company, the pretty green grass may be only a temporary illusion. I doubt it will be worth destroying your family for in the end.

Hopefully there are good reasons you chose to be with your spouse. Think of all the positive attributes that you love. Reflect back to see if *you are giving* to the relationship as much *as you want* from the relationship.

Maybe you can make the grass turn greener right there where you are at!

Tip: If your relationship or family means something to you, don't even go down a path that might lead to you doing something to destroy it. If there are problems in the relationship, work on fixing the problems so that there is comfort and security inside the relationship instead of either of the you seeking acceptance and gratification elsewhere.

You and your family deserve that peace and happiness and a lifelong companionship that a strong healthy relationship could and should offer.

Besides, it will make you live longer, healthier and be more prosperous who would want to destroy that!

I have seen many more happily married truckers and wives than unhappy. You can be happy too with a little work, the right attitude and the right partner.

www.lifeasatrucker.com

Advice For Single Truckers

Reading all I covered in the previous chapter should be enough for you to understand why my advice for single drivers is.....

Stay single!

At least for the first year or so. By then you will have a better idea of what direction you will take in trucking. You avoid having to deal with so many issues, especially like spending more time at home. Obviously, you just can't make money as a trucker and also spend a lot of time at home. You have to drive to make money.

Plus as a single driver you can really focus on making yourself a better person while you have all the alone time on the open highway. That way, when you get in a relationship later you really are ready to be a better companion to someone even if you are out over the road.

Enjoy your freedom while you save your money, get out of debt, build your credit, get experience and learn more about the ins and outs of the industry.

Better position yourself to be able to enjoy your relationships (and life) in the future by paying your dues now. Determine what your plans will be for getting out of the truck or retiring early. Or maybe just spend time at home the way you want. Supposed you have other aspirations, hobbies or businesses you want to pursue when you get home. If you are in a relationship either those plans or the relationship will suffer. (Unless you have a very special woman, who also understands and support the entrepreneurial spirit... and you are very energetic!)

Many trucker's wives say that the driver doesn't want to do anything when he comes home. They are frustrated because of this, which is understandable. Point is, you only have so much time. So think about where you are in life and if a serious relationship is right for you at this period in time.

When you are in a comfortable place with a clear vision of what steps you will take to get to where you want to be, then make yourself available for a relationship.

Your spouse will be more confident and secure in being with a trucker that has a plan in action. She can actually see your big picture when you say, "Baby I won't be out on the road for ever". This confident and sense of security makes it easier to have a strong healthy relationship with less drama, surprises, or stress.

It also makes it easier to do realistic family planning when taking the relationship to the next level. For instance, if your money is straight, you can afford to take time off early enough to make some of the important dates.

Tip: Some people would rather not be on the road as a trucker with a family at home. Knowing this, they still never plan ahead and set goals of how they will transition out of the truck. Consider this, and make plans accordingly. Set yourself up to leave trucking if you want.

If you plan now you can set yourself up to drive for 5 or 10 years and then only drive if and when you want. You can start and build your own business while you are driving either online or at home using your skills and knowledge.

I am working on both. Internet marketing, you can check it out at www.earnwhileyoulearn.ws (where of course you can join up if you so desire) and also editing video, graphic design, customizing photos and related creative uses of the computer. By the time I find a wife and have kids I will be able to actually charge for my services and make money at home instead of being out over the road.

I talk to people all the time who want to stop driving and can't because of no other way to earn money immediately. Also, more commonly than you would assume, there are many drivers who need to make extra money while they are driving and that puts a strain on the family too.

So don't put off developing a way to make extra money.

Still Interested in Becoming A Trucker?
Do You Want a Job or a Career?

What's the difference you say?

A job in my mind is where you spend the day watching the clock wishing it was time to go. You may have a few benefits and that helps you to stay for a while but your not happy. You do as little as you have to and they pay you as little as they can for it.

If the company has to downsize you will probably be the first to go because you don't like your boss and he/she doesn't really care for your either. Plus, they know you are only doing a mediocre job at best. The ongoing stress makes you hate it there.

A career on the other hand is a job where you choose to remain where you are employed because you enjoy the work, the people and the work environment.

www.lifeasatrucker.com

You appreciate the company and the company appreciates you. **The company views you as an asset** because you are dependable, responsible, trustworthy and you have a positive attitude. You get along well with the people there and the customers of the company. Because of your job performance and record you will be one of the last people canned if the company has to downsize. You are happy at work even on bad days.

Now, which situation would you like to find yourself in?

Tip: No matter if you become a trucker or decide trucking is not for you, always work for your boss like you would want an employee to work for you. During the recession a lot of people were let go from their jobs who should have been let go long before the recession. Also, you never know who is watching your work performance. You may get a raise, promotion or even a job offer from another company all because of your attitude and work ethic.

www.lifeasatrucker.com

Here is How To Make Trucking A Career

To make trucking a career you handle yourself with the long term big picture in mind. You want to make the most money you can as a driver. You want to be happy and you want to have options. If your company is not treating you right after you get experience, you want to be able to go to a better company. If you make decisions with those thoughts in mind you are most likely to make choices that will make your vision for the future a reality.

No company is perfect. But there are thousands of companies. Handle yourself in a way that you are desirable as an employee for a company that will treat you right so you won't be stuck without options.

So what you need to do is practice what we mentioned earlier....be responsible, have a positive attitude, communicate and follow company and D.O.T rules and regulations.

www.lifeasatrucker.com

Tips to help Make Trucking a Great Career....

- ## Don't Jump From Company to Company

You don't want to hop from trucking company to trucking company. As I said earlier, no company is going to be perfect. Everyday is not going to be good, every load is not going to be good, every week is not going to be good.

So the minute something you don't like happens don't just quit. (Also, resist going off on the people in the office or feeling like they are doing you wrong. Don't take these things personally)

Don't leave and go to another company just because you can. Do that enough and soon you won't be able to.

You will hear drivers talking about how many different trucking jobs they have had and that it didn't keep them from getting another job. You'll continue to get hired by other companies for a while, but do you think the best companies will hire someone who jumps from company to company?

Companies who will hire that driver will likely be like shark smelling blood in the water. They know that the driver has limited options so they pay him peanuts and run him like a machine. He and the company are destined to fail.

Why?

Because a company that will hire him is more likely to try running him illegally and he is more likely to do it knowing that not many other companies will hire him. He ends up with more violations meaning even less options and eventually he is unqualified to drive a commercial vehicle anywhere. Not to mention that running this way without proper rest is excessive wear and tear on the body and so could lead to poor health. On top of that, it could lead to eventual depression from realizing that you are stuck at a job you hate dealing with people who don't care about drivers. Your stuck with no options for switching to a better company.

Do NOT become this driver!

Hang in there at your trucking job as long as you can to get that year of experience. At least wait long enough to see if you are being mistreated or if a problem you have is an isolated incident. If you see the same types of problems reoccurring be professional in how you talk to someone about it.

Maybe they don't know, or don't understand.

The first person you should talk to if you feel you are being handled wrong is the person who is handling you wrong. Give him or her a chance to either explain and/or correct the behavior.

Keep a log of these events and document the responses and changes (or lack thereof) based on your complaints.

If there is no satisfactory changes, keep going up your chain of command.

Hopefully you will soon be taken seriously and the issue will be addressed. If there are illegal, unsafe, inappropriate actions, you may want to speak to an arbitrator, the D.O.T., E.E.O.C, or an attorney to decide what course of action is best to take next.

- **Take Care of Your CDL And Job Performance**
  The company you are at will have less trouble with the D.O.T. If their drivers don't get tickets or log book violations. You will have less trouble too. If the company your employed by has a poor safety record the D.O.T. is inclined to pull you over and check you out more frequently.

www.lifeasatrucker.com

Keep your logbook inspection ready and don't speed. Be sure to have your medical card and CDL on you. Be sure to check your tires for exposed wires, shallow depth and low pressure. Check for leaks and blown lights. Check the other items on the inspections checklist. Many violations now will not only go on record for your company but on record for the driver too.

After you rack up a certain number of points within a certain period of time you will be unqualified to drive and no company can hire you. You better believe the closer you are to the threshold the harder time you will have getting a good job. That means you don't have to be disqualified to be negatively affected.

You'll hear complaints about all of this. Drivers will lose jobs and companies will get shut down. More than likely, it all needed to happen. Eventually, the industry will be more respected and drivers may see higher pay because of higher standards.

So let's recap....

The more violations you have the more you will be inspected and the more you are inspected the more likely it is that they will find something wrong which means you will get even more violations. This is a cycle that you don't want to be a part of.

- **Check Your Driving Habits**

Watch how you drive. Be courteous to your fellow drivers and to four wheelers. They are going to act a fool with you sometimes but you are the professional they are not.   Work on your patience for other drivers. You will be cut off and cursed out but learn to smile and just let it go. Take deep breaths and count to 10 (or 50) to reach a calm state of being. Keep a safe following distance.

Simple things like signaling properly prior to making a turn or changing a lane is helpful to everyone on the highway.

www.lifeasatrucker.com

You will be amazed at how many people don't use their turn signals or use it improperly.

Some drivers will wait until after they apply the brakes and slow down to turn on the turn signal. There is no need to put on your turn signal at that point, it obvious that your going to be turning.

When you are driving in the city and you are coming up on a red light, if pulling all the way up to the car ahead will block someone in a driveway, pause long enough to let the driver out before closing the gap. It's no skin off your back and the kind gesture goes a long way. If it is the only entrance or exit to a business and your not obstructing the road, leave the driveway open until the light turns green instead of blocking it. Smile and wave to the people that comes through that they may go and tell their friend how a nice trucker was to him/her to let them out on a busy street.

www.lifeasatrucker.com

This seems small but it's many small acts like these that helps change the way truckers are perceived and therefor change the way they are treated.

Example: So when we encounter these people that truckers have been courteous to on the highway, they are more likely to let us over when we notice the building we are looking for at the last minute.

Also they will give us more respect or courtesy so as not to do things such as cut us off by pulling in front of us only to slam the brake and turn or exit.

***Tip:** The way we treat each other always matters and it comes back around at some point, sometimes directly and sometimes indirectly, consciously or subconsciously on the highway and off. Trucker or not.*

This realization by experts, gurus and news media will become part of common conversation one day soon.
It all matters.

www.lifeasatrucker.com

- **Treat your equipment like it is your own**

Pay attention to your truck. When it changes the way it drives, usually that means something is wrong. Alignments and other front end problems may develop easily because of the size and abundance of potholes on some highways. Of course, hitting the curb might cause you problems too!

Belts in the tires break, balance weights fly off, and bearings get worn out, they all cause a change in the way a truck drives. Usually causes a vibration.

If you notice something is different about how your truck drives, take it in to the shop, don't wait until it falls apart. Waiting could be unsafe and could create a bigger problem that costs a lot more to get fixed later.

www.lifeasatrucker.com

Some small problems like putting in fuses or light bulbs may be something you can do yourself and get reimbursed for by the company instead of wasting time and money in the shop. Some companies have policies that are specific about how such things will be handled. You'll have check after choosing a company.

If your truck is filthy get it washed. Your company will discuss their policy for truck washes. Some may want it only done at terminals. Other companies will pay for washes over the road or they may reimburse you   when you get back in or immediately after.

A filthy appearance may not only influence how your truck and company is perceived by the public, but it may also influence the D.O.T. Officer to want to see if your log book is just as ugly.

Take your truck in for oil changes on time and report codes on your dash. Insist that important problems are fixed such as air leaks and fluid leaks.

When you bring a trailer in, don't leave the trailer parked on the yard without reporting problems because you are getting rid of the trailer. The next driver shouldn't have to deal with a problem that could have been fixed while the trailer was sitting on the yard.

Remember what you do comes back around, you don't want to pick up one of these trailers so don't leave one there for someone else to pick up.

Tip: *Having a good work ethic saves the company, the other drivers, and you time and money in the long run and makes the highways safer for everyone.   Combine that with a positive attitude and you have stronger company and more secure job. Take care of your equipment, your customers, and handle your responsibilities.*

Hopefully the higher profit margins the company will reward good drivers higher pay and better benefits.

www.lifeasatrucker.com

Eating a Healthy Diet as a Trucker

You want to keep your health in mind as a truck driver. It's easy to pop into the truck stop and pick up the fastest junk food available. The excuse is made all of the time that you can't eat healthy over the road. It's a lie!

There are always options for something reasonably healthy at truck stops. Plus, a lot of truck stops now have Subways in them. (Choose the wheat bread instead of white). Some truck stops even have salads prepared in plastic containers, which you could easily add your tuna to or not. All truck stops have peanuts, most have bananas and both of them makes quick healthy snacks if your short on time.

The best way to eat healthy is to bring your own food with you. It's cheaper and faster than eating in the truck stop.

www.lifeasatrucker.com

Beans, tuna, cereal and fruits will cost less per meal than anything bought out of the truck stop. I lost more than 35lbs with this diet while over the road as a trucker.

Taking your own food can be quicker because instead of going to the truck stop to eat, you can pull off in a rest area. It's quicker to park and no lines to wait in. The bonus is that you won't be tempted by the cakes, cookies and candy bars sitting at the checkout counter calling your name!

What we eat is important but also how much we eat. We must get out of the mindset of stuffing ourselves with food at each meal or either meal.

This feasting is done especially at buffets where it is natural to want to get your money's worth. It really isn't a good idea and is in fact costly in the long run when you factor in obesity and the diseases that comes along with that familiar habit.

www.lifeasatrucker.com

Help your body be healthier by eating smaller portions more frequently. Eating smaller portions helps to boost and regulate your metabolism so that you actually burn more calories and fat even while at rest. It also allows your body to operate more efficiently.

Anything that you can do to help your body operate more efficiently is going to have long term positive effect on your health. Doing the opposite, obviously delivers the opposite results, poor health and increased suffering.

Truckers are prime candidates for heart disease, high blood, diabetes, and sleep apnea due to constant temptation of junk food and lack of exercise. We must be intentional to change this reality.

Since drivers were not taking care of their own health, government has stepped in. Health has now become an important factor that will also be evaluated and used for your Safety Score.
It's sad that it takes regulation for us to take better care of our bodies, but that's where we are.

www.lifeasatrucker.com

Can You Get Exercise As a Trucker?

Of course you can get exercise as a trucker. You won't be
hitting the gym for most of your exercise but you can still
get a great workout. All you have to do is be intentional
with your activities through out the day. You can start by
doing crunches or sit ups and push ups right on the bunk
before you ever get out of bed. The mattresses that
comes in the truck are perfect for it. You also can do leg
lifts while on your sides, on your stomach, and on your
back. That's an energizing way to get going before eating
your healthy breakfast.

Through out the day you can do simple things such as
isolating your muscles groups while washing your
windows, mirrors, sweeping your trailer out, etc. Stretch
in full range of motion each direction and feel those
muscles working. You can also do squats, shadow box, or
do push ups when waiting at the fuel pumps or while
getting loaded or unloaded.

www.lifeasatrucker.com

At some companies you can get paid to load or unload yourself. That's like getting paid to exercise.

You can walk while your getting loaded or unloaded if you are at a company that allows you to be outside of the truck on their property (some don't). You can walk or jog around the truck stop when you park for the night. Park at the far end in of the lot at truck stops. Try shadow boxing or make your own routine to music to do in the evening after driving or in the morning to start your day.

(I saw that a driver was about to do a complete book about exercise in the truck in 2011 eleven. I will find that information and have it available on the website.)

Tip: Some people will circle the parking lot over and over trying to park at the front door. Why waste that time being lazy? Get parked quicker and get your exercise by simply going to the far end parking spaces and take a walk to the building.

www.lifeasatrucker.com

You can even take dumbbells with you over the road to do more traditional weight lifting exercises if you want.

As you can see, there is no excuse for not getting exercise or achieving better health. It's a matter of choice followed by action. Like so many other things in life if you want it, it's there, you just have to be willing to put forth the time, effort, sacrifice and have the discipline to make it part of your life.

We spend a lot of money on medicine to address symptoms we experience which comes from medical issues that would not exist if we lived a healthier lifestyle.

Decide that you will intentionally be a health conscious person now and especially should you choose to become a truck driver.

Why is it so important to get exercise as a trucker?

1. We spend hours sitting for years while being bounced up and down and blocking circulation so it is important to help our bodies as much as possible to cope with the beating.

2. It's easier to start those good habits from the beginning, than it is to correct bad habits later. Even sometimes after they have already caused serious harm to your health.

3. Medical problems will cost you money and time off from work which may cut into your family plans, financial freedom or retirement plans.

www.lifeasatrucker.com

Downtime Over The Road

There are many constructive, positive, convenient and free or cheap ways to spend your time and make it work for you especially if you decide it is in your best interest to avoid going out in order to stay out of trouble or save money.

Spend time reading, writing, researching your family history, researching trucking or any other subject that interests you on the internet.

Reading and or writing helps to keep your mind sharp and sparks creativity which can then be used to your advantage, in other ways. This is a powerful way to spend your down time.

www.lifeasatrucker.com

Build a website or a blog about your hobbies or journeys on the road. You can take the information about what you already know and turn it into a website business which you can work on in your down time to supplement your income. It may help you get off the road early all while helping others. It's also a fun way to share time and focus with your significant other providing an additional way to connect.

I am building a website to help promote businesses in my local community at home.   I use SBI because they train you how to properly design and promote. (I am also an affiliate, which is another way you can make money while on the road.)

During downtime you can also join online trucking communities like the one I am building at social.lifeasatrucker.com. Come and connect with us, share stories from the road, network with others, add your blog or discussion to the site.

The internet really opens up a whole new world for having fun, learning, making money, socializing and making the most out of free time wherever you are.

Don't forget you can also connect with family at home with services such as Skype. You can use also stream live video especially cool if you have kids at home.

With this free time you can also choose to further educate yourself so that you are empowered to do things beyond trucking even while out over the road.

Supposed you learned about photography and developed your skills while on the road taking pictures during down time across the country to send back to family at home. They will love feeling connected from seeing some of what you see on the road and you will be developing a skill that you may be able to use to make money at some point when you are ready to get out of the truck and be home with the family. Photograph weddings or other events. Photograph high value items for insurance documentation.

Maybe you will use the skills on the road to earn extra money while driving. Take picture of drivers and their truck. You'll see the ones who may go for it, big fancy super sleepers painted up. Some drivers spend a lot of time and money on their rig. Catch them fresh out of the truck wash and they may be easy happy customers.

If you are thinking about becoming an owner operator why not read about running a small business. Learn about brokering freight. Learn about different aspects of trucking that will be beneficial in your next potential move within the trucking industry.

What does it take to become an owner operator?
Is it beneficial to have your own authority or not?
How do you get your own authority?
You can learn this and more online, free!

Your plans for the future should help dictate how you spend a lot of the free time you have while you are on the road.

We all pay our dues to get to where we want to be in life, we either pay them now or we pay them later but they must be paid. The sooner the dues are paid, the sooner we sit back and enjoy the fruits of our labor.

Going Out On The Town

If your going out, you don't want to stay out so late that you will not be able to perform the next day. You also don't want alcohol on your breath and you don't want a hangover the next day. Keep that in mind if you go out. Remember the track record your creating and your plans for achieving your goals. These thoughts will help you to make better decisions when the time comes.

Some people remain 100 percent in control when they go out. Others may have weaknesses in any of several areas that could result in poor decisions. If you can't leave the club or bar until it closes when you go out then you might not want to go out. If you know you often make poor decisions after having a few drinks, you may not want to drink. If you know you can't control your drinking when you go out, you might not want to go out at all!

 www.lifeasatrucker.com

There are many options for spending your off time other than clubs and bars. Sometimes there will be bowling alleys, museums, amusement parks, movie theaters, malls, casinos, etc.

If your money is tight, spending your money on these activities routinely will keep you from saving money. Will that help you to reach your goals? What is your purpose for becoming a trucker?   Stay in control of your destiny. All things in moderation.

If you find yourself constantly getting cash advances and it's due to how you spend your down time you might want to reflect on how this will impact what your trying to achieve with your trucking career. This way you can make some adjustments before you look back 3 years down the road saying I wish or, I woulda, coulda, shoulda. You don't want to be out on the road spending every dime that you make without saving and investing in your family or your future. Speaking of money...

www.lifeasatrucker.com

How Much Money Does the
Average Trucker Make?

What a trucker makes varies. Some drivers get paid percentage, most get paid by the mile. There are thousands of trucking companies so there are a few other compensations models that exists and variants from the average pay scales. The type of trucking jobs makes a difference in your pay also.

For most drivers starting out in the career, you will be pulling a dry van hauling general freight for a large trucking company unless you know someone who is going to give you a break hauling something else.

The **salary of those entry level trucking jobs range from about $25,000 to $35,000** for the first year of driving for most truckers starting in today's economy. During training your pay will not be what most people expect, probably between $250 and $500 per week.

www.lifeasatrucker.com

After training and getting out over the road your pay will probably be more like $500 to $700 per week. Take this into account if you need a certain amount of money to cover your bills and you thought you were that you were going to cover them by making a lot of money starting off as a trucker. It's just not going to happen from the start.

If you have a trucking company in mind, ask drivers from that company what their average monthly pay is. The reason I said monthly is because weekly pay will vary, one higher than average week usually means the next week is lower than average so a monthly average is likely to be a more accurate figure to use for comparing driver's pay at different companies.

You also have to ask where a driver lives and how often he/she goes home. If you want to be home often, your pay will be less than another driver who stays out on the road or who lives right off an interstate that is heavily traveled by that company.

With each year of driving for the first 5 years or so you will be able to make more and more money if, you keep your record clean from tickets, log book violations, and accidents.

After five years or so if you cap out your pay at the company you are at, decide if you will stay, or go to a company that only hires experienced and seasoned drivers with clean records where you will likely make more money.

Before switching companies be sure to consider the benefits other than pay per mile. If you have wife and kids your dental and health insurance coverage and expense may be more valuable to you than pay per mile.

Also consider how well you get along with the people in your office and how skilled they are at keeping you moving. Before switching talk to drivers at the company that you are considering going to about sitting and waiting on loads. Compare this with miles per month he states. There should be a correlation.

www.lifeasatrucker.com

Higher Paying Trucking Companies

So what are some of the higher paying company driving jobs I mentioned earlier? Experienced and seasoned drivers with clean records has more options with better companies who will only hire drivers with 2 or more years experience. Sometimes these companies require a driver to be above a minimum age too. They want maturity.

They usually want a clean MVR and criminal record. For sure now you will also have to have good safety score.

Most of these companies manufacture their own products or distribute goods to their own stores. They run their own trucking operation using their own trucks. (Some use owner operators too). That means the shipper and receivers are all part of the same team so their expenses for trucking is less than the regular common carriers. In order to make the operations as successful as possible they obviously need proven dependable drivers.

Pay attention as you ride the highway and you will see these company trucks promoting their brand or products with painted trailers used as a moving billboard.

Talk to these drivers and collect information about getting on after getting experience in case the company you start off with does not treat you right or doesn't pay you what you are worth.

That means taking care of your driving and employment record.

Make The Most Money In Trucking

First let's go back and recap some of the things that I mentioned earlier. If you were paying attention, you would realize that each of the topics we talked about will allow you to make and/or keep more money.

To start with, **saving money is making money**!

Which means, do what you can to avoid throwing money away or wasting money.

It also means, make the tough decisions that you need to for your situation. If you don't it could easily cost you.

Tip*: There is no magic trick to making money, it's a matter of the way you think, the way you plan, and the discipline you use to carry out those plans.*

Ok, Ok, Ok let's get into the recap....

Here some points to remember...

- Make sure you and your spouse's situation is suitable for the trucking lifestyle.(or it could cost)
- Do your research to determine what company is a good match for you. Location, pay, benefits, etc
- Develop and maintain a positive attitude to help think rationally and make better decisions
- Make sure that you and your spouse budget to remain aware of your financial condition
- Develop Good Habits
- Plan Ahead – Save money and avoid emergencies
- Keep Your Record Clean
- Take Care of Your Health

Obviously, handling those things properly will automatically result in you ending up with more money. Not handling them properly could not only cost you financially but also in pain and suffering mentally, medically, socially or in all four ways.

Hauling Specialized Freight to Make More Money in Trucking

Now to make more money behind the wheel you will need to specialize as a driver. Specialize means to drive something other than a dry van. There are many types of truck driving jobs, some pay more than others.

Flatbed and reefer are the next closest thing to dry van. It is the easiest specialized trucking job for new drivers to get in to. They do pay a little more money because there is more responsibility.

Any freight that must be kept at a specific temperature will be hauled in a refrigerated trailer. You must monitor the reefer unit to make sure the trailer reefer unit is set to specified temperature and maintains no more or less than the allowed temperature window.

www.lifeasatrucker.com

Flat beds also pay more than dry van. The flat bed has several different components of extra responsibility and work. It's not for every driver. Some duties will include securing the load, sometimes with nail, hammer and wood (as Keith will show you on the video), tarping sometimes, being able to judge weight distribution of odd objects, etc.

You can actually start off with reefer or flatbed if you do enough searching for companies who will hire new recruits and train them.

There are many specialized carries for different items. You could also specialize in hauling cars or boats. You will need experience for those jobs too in most cases. Of course they too pay more than dry van.

One of the highest paying trucking jobs is heavy hauling.
Heavy Hauling pays a lot more money because the driver
has a **lot** more responsibility.

Special routing, load security, and attention to detail is
critical to carrying out your job successfully. Some people
are not cut out for this type of work.

Van lines pays pretty well plus you get good exercise. You
can't be afraid of physical work because moving furniture
several days a week in and out of homes or businesses is
hard work but it has its benefits. More money and you
stay in shape. You may be sore for the first few weeks if
you are not used to physical activity, but there is nothing
like getting a workout on the clock.

Tip: *All you have to do is pay attention to the customized*
tractors you see on the highway. It's obvious there is big
money in doing what they are doing. Many of them are
owner operators but the same companies often have good
opportunities for company drivers. Talk to these drivers.

www.lifeasatrucker.com

Can you Make More Money As an Owner Operator?

You will make more money as an <u>owner operator</u>. The question is will you end up with more money at the end of the year as an owner operator when compared to company drivers. The answer is, it depends...

Owner operators will make more money than a **new company driver no question** if you manage your money properly, use an accountant that is familiar with trucking and you have dependable equipment pulling decent paying freight. But, I don't recommend becoming an o/o as a brand new driver. Wait at least a 1yr.

Once you get years of experience, it's possible to get a company job with good benefits to match what an owner operator pulling a dry van with regular freight makes after taxes. By then you will have learned enough about trucking to decide if owner operator is what you want.

www.lifeasatrucker.com

However, one of the key benefits of becoming an owner operator is that you can make the money faster and hold on to it until quarterly taxes are due. This is useful if you have side projects going on. You must be careful to be able to pay the taxes.

This also means you can spend more time at home in theory and make the same or more money as a company driver depending on how much you want to run, which will be based partially on your monthly expenses for your equipment unless you save and buy outright.

Another key benefit as an owner operator is that you will have more freedom of choice as a trucker in the loads you take and where you run, depending on whether you have your own authority or lease on to a company that allows you to operate that way. Landstar is a good company to lease to.

Specialized hauling as an owner operator pays more than pulling dry van and considerably more than a company driver. With this you can make money.

Of course you really want to know about the principles of conducting business if you want to be an owner operator. One of the common reasons that owner operators fail is because of lack of understanding in running a business.

For example, you must save to pay quarterly taxes and other expenses that a company drivers doesn't have to deal with. Some drivers blow their money planning on paying the taxes later. If you spend that money and don't save for repairs then the truck breaks down you have to either fix the truck or pay your taxes, buy fuel, etc that's a problem.

Many drivers don't see becoming owner operator as running a business which also leads to many failures. These are the guys who will most commonly tell you to not buy a truck because you can't make money.

 www.lifeasatrucker.com

As a company driver handle your job like it is your truck and your own business and that will make actually being an owner operator second nature should you decide to take the leap.

Cutting cost when you can like not idling the truck unnecessarily, planning where to stop for fuel where the prices are the cheapest with in the state puts you in good practice. The more you understand about mechanics the better you are at knowing what is wrong with your truck so you can determine when and where you need to get service done.

When you break down in a company truck, ask the mechanic questions about the breakdown. Is it something you caused, could it have been prevented, is it normal wear and tear? What work would you recommend me to have done to this truck with this mileage if it were mine? What problems are you aware of about this engine, this transmission, or this truck?

www.lifeasatrucker.com

These questions gives you knowledge and insight about not only the truck you are driving but maybe a truck you are considering buying in the future.

Tip: *Remember as an owner operator all the responsibility and expenses fall on you so you will want to study about becoming an owner operator and prepare financially while you are getting your experience as a company driver so that you are properly positioned when it's time for you to make your move if you choose to do so.*

www.lifeasatrucker.com

Some Advantages of Trucking

1. No boss breathing down your neck watching your every move.

2. You get to see the country in which you live for free. In fact your getting paid.

3. If you take a job in which you load and unload you are getting paid to exercise.

4. While working you have the time to do some self reflecting and <u>allow trucking to help you become a better person.</u>

5. You can get good benefits with the right company.

6. You can make a decent amount of money without spending a fortune in training.

7. You can take trucking as far as you want to go, you can buy a truck, 2, 5. You can start a trucking company with a fleet or you can just be the boss of you and 1 truck.

8. You don't have to spend your gas money on going back and forth to work every day!

www.lifeasatrucker.com

Some Disadvantages Trucking

1. You will be away from home from 2-3 weeks at a time at most companies. At some companies you may be gone as long as 3 to 5 weeks.
2. Even scheduled home time doesn't always guarantee that you will make it back home sometimes.
3. You'll miss some important family dates eventually.
4. If not handled properly, trucking could cause damage to your relationships.
5. If you don't handle your money properly, you could spend all the money you make
6. If you are not careful, you could easily end up out of shape and overweight
7. If you are not cut out for the lifestyle you can also become <u>depressed</u>, <u>stressed</u>, and/or <u>lonely</u>

Additional Tips Should You Decide to Become a Trucker

1. Always park in designated spaces. I know you will see trucks parked everywhere including on ramps. It is up to the D.O.T. Whether they want to write you up for parking on the ramps. Truck stops are tricky too. If your truck is hit and your not in a parking space you will be blamed for the accident.

2. Practice your backing. When you get to a truck stop in the evening that has empty spaces, don't take advantage of the empty lot by pulling through. You are missing an opportunity. Take advantage of the empty lot by practicing your backing into a parking space just as if a truck was parked on each side. Do it a few times times, but don't get carried away! Do it again at your next opportunity. Even practice at a real dock if you arrive at a deserted delivery or pick up early or while they are on lunch.

3. Always leave early to get to your destinations. You can't control some of the things that may happen in route like storms, accidents, break downs but you can control how much cushion time you start with.

   Leaving at the last minute to make an appointment leaves you little room for these unplanned events that will happen when you least expect it. Plan on it.

4. Save up to 3 months of your household expenses before you and your spouse began spending money based on speculation that you will be gainfully employed or making more money soon. You never know what the future holds and you don't know what emergencies will arise at the home front. Being prepared helps to keep you from dealing with the emergencies and crisis situations. You will hear drivers selling equipment while on the road. Sometimes that is a sign of poor money management and it isn't fun for him or his spouse at home.

5. Never abandon your equipment or your load no matter what the situation. You'll be black balled.

Did I say NEVER abandon your equipment or a load!?! That will get you black balled by trucking companies and make it difficult to be hired as a driver. Just think about it.

Who would want to hire a person who leaves $100,000 or more worth of someone else's stuff somewhere other than where it is supposed to be. Excuses as to why you did it will not fly. Even what seems to be good excuses including emergencies will fall on deaf ears when trying to get hired somewhere else.

Well, obviously it depends on the emergency but if its truly serious most good companies will give you authorization to take truck to nearest terminal if they can't route you to your home terminal.

Even if you have permission, get it in writing or record it with a voice recorder so if it goes on your DAC report you have proof it was authorized. Remember an emergency to you might not be a REAL emergency in the eyes of the company.

6. Never leave the scene of an accident. This is probably the second worse thing that you can do to get black balled.

Don't Be A Slob

Something else I want to point out since I have your attention is to not be like those guys who throw trash or piss bottles on the ground. No matter where you park, never disrespect people's property. You will hear drivers complain about different businesses or property owners that don't want trucks parking on their lot.

It's simple to see why. Sometimes you can look on the ground where we are allowed to park and you see how nasty and thoughtless some people are. Probably some of the same people doing the complaining about not being allowed to park in some places are the one's that throws trash on the ground including piss bottles.

Please don't be one of those types of driver (or person for that matter). Again, that does nothing to help our image. It does fit neatly in the stereotypical negative thoughts that people may already associate truckers with. The same thoughts that wreak havoc on relationships.

www.lifeasatrucker.com

Conclusion

You should now have enough insight about trucking to make an informed decision about whether to become a trucker or not. Better informed people on the road means drivers with better driving habits and better attitudes. This means safer highways and a more pleasant work environment.

Eventually, better quality drivers with better attitudes will get treated better across the board. We also will develop an improved image allowing the public to see us in a more positive light which more closely represents the majority of truckers.

This will help all truckers and especially those in relationships because believe it or not how we are perceived has an influence on people's thoughts.

www.lifeasatrucker.com

These thoughts could easily come into play with a driver's relationship at home. They can be generated with the spouse or with the people that she associates with or confides in about her relationship. The most common input that someone will have to give to her is more than likely to be something negative about truckers. That's all they know.

Truckers who desire to change that negativity have to not do what is expected by society. We have to rebuild our reputation one driver at a time.   Same is true with any group you belong to. If you want to be treated differently than what you know people assume, you must remain consciously aware of your actions. Check yourself. Are you behaving as they assume or do you shine in spite of their negative perceptions. Will you be a part of positive change or an addition to the problems?

You are going to help me make that negative stereotype disappear right?

We hope to help change the face of the trucking industry by enabling drivers to make better decisions in trucking and in life on the road and off. I hope that you will help this movement first by thinking through whether you are really the type of person in the right situation suitable for becoming a happy, prosperous, professional driver.

I wish you the best of luck in whatever direction you decide to take with your life. If you get a chance come check us out at www.lifeasatrucker.com to get even more information about trucking or maybe find a trucking school to get started!

Best Wishes,
Hervy A.K.A The Crazy Trucker

If you decide that trucking is not for you, find another happening career at my website www.career-change-blog.org

Questions to ask truckers or companies that your interested in?

(Write your answers on the next pages)

Numbers 6 – 10 is for your questions.

1. How often are you able to get home?

2. How much do you make a month?

3. What benefits do you have?

4. What type of equipment does your company have?

5. How often do you come through.....(whatever highway is closest to your home)

6.

7.

8.

9.

10.

Company Name	Q 1 Home Time	Q2 Pay	Q3 Benefits	Q4 Equipment	Q5 Rider Program?

Company Name	Q6 Home Time	Q7 Pay	Q8 Benefits	Q9 Equipment	Q10 Rider Program?

Company Name	Q1 Home time	Q2 Pay	Q3 Benefits	Q4 Equipment	Q5 Rider Program

Company Name	Q6	Q7	Q8	Q9	Q10

Company Name	Q6	Q7	Q8	Q9	Q10

Notes Page 1

www.lifeasatrucker.com

Notes Page 2

Notes Page 3

Want to be a famous Trucker?

Well, maybe famous is an overstatement but we will definitely

be choosing drivers for our documentary

about

Life As A Trucker.

Featuring possibly you and other real drivers about their experience.

If you are interested in being a part of the documentary which covers

a person's decision to become a trucker (and the spouses reaction)

and into his/her first year with interview updates. Check out

<u>doc.lifeasatrucker.org</u> for more details and information.

Much Success and Happiness!